Be a CITIZEN SCIENTIST!

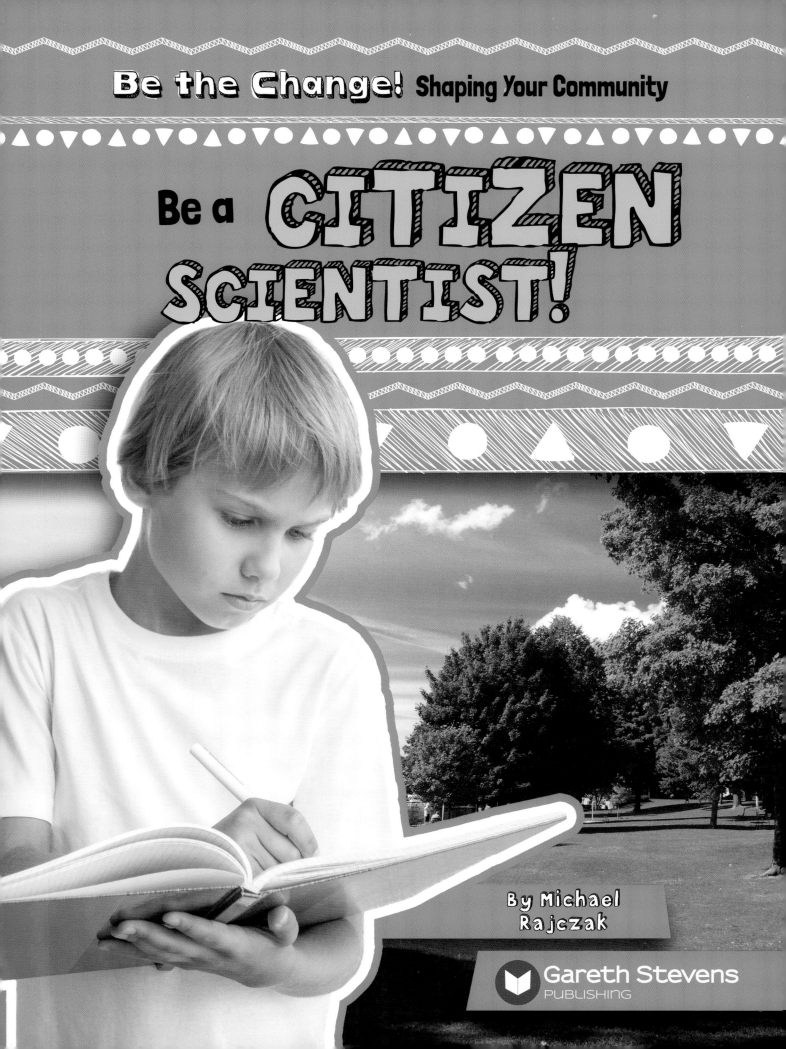

By Michael Rajczak

Gareth Stevens
PUBLISHING

Please visit our website, www.garethstevens.com. For a free color catalog of all our high-quality books, call toll free 1-800-542-2595 or fax 1-877-542-2596.

Cataloging-in-Publication Data

Names: Rajczak, Michael
Title: Be a citizen scientist! / Michael Rajczak.
Description: New York : Gareth Stevens Publishing, 2019. | Series: Be the change! shaping your community | Includes index.
Identifiers: LCCN ISBN 9781538219973 (pbk.) | ISBN 9781538219959 (library bound) | ISBN 9781538219980 (6 pack)
Subjects: LCSH: Science–Juvenile literature. | Science–Methodology–Juvenile literature.
Classification: LCC Q163.R36 2019 | DDC 500.2072'1–dc23

Published in 2019 by
Gareth Stevens Publishing
111 East 14th Street, Suite 349
New York, NY 10003

Designer: Laura Bowen
Editor: Joan Stoltman

Photo credits: Cover, p. 1 (main) Veja/Shutterstock.com; cover, p. 1 (background) Jack Aiello/Shutterstock.com; p. 5 (top) Bartosz Budrewicz/Shutterstock.com; p. 5 (bottom) Photodiem/Shutterstock.com; p. 7 Jausa/Shutterstock.com; p. 9 Ariel Skelley/DigitalVision/Getty Images; p. 10 feathercollector/Shutterstock.com; p. 11 Pavlo Lys/Shutterstock.com; p. 12 AlphaBoom/Shutterstuck.com; p. 13 My Life Graphic/Shutterstock.com; p. 17 Chumack John/Science Source/Getty Images; pp. 19, 29 Hero Images/Getty Images; p. 20 D.Bond/Shutterstock.com; p. 21 Westend61/Getty Images; p. 22 5 second Studio/Shutterstock.com; p. 23 LightField Studios/Shutterstock.com; p. 25 (top) KC Lens and Footage/Shutterstock.com; p. 25 (bottom) Flashpop/Taxi/Getty Images; p. 27 Hill Street Studios/Eric Raptosh/Blend Images/Getty Images; p. 28 TeddyGraphics/Shutterstock.com.

Printed in the United States of America

CPSIA compliance information: Batch #CS18GS: For further information contact Gareth Stevens, New York, New York at 1-800-542-2595.

CONTENTS

Words in the glossary appear in **bold** type the first time they are used in the text.

What Is a Citizen Scientist?

Science is the study of the natural world through observations and experiments. Weather, oceans, and rocks are part of Earth science. Life science includes plants and animals, and physical science deals with matter and energy. Science is all around us!

Has something ever caught your interest and made you curious? To learn more, you may have done some exploration, observation, and careful study called research. Reporting your findings makes you a citizen scientist! Part of being a citizen scientist is collecting data. The other part is reporting this data to a working scientist or science group.

Part of Something Bigger

There are many science groups around the world that rely on citizen scientists' data. They use the data to track the movement and numbers of animals or make discoveries about Earth and even space! This book will introduce you to many such projects and tell you how to become a citizen scientist yourself!

Ruby-throated hummingbirds migrate, or move to another place to mate and feed, each spring and fall. By reporting hummingbird sightings, citizen scientists can help scientists discover changes in the migration timing of the **species**.

A Group Effort

For most of human history, people couldn't make a living as full-time scientists. A person who made important discoveries was often someone who collected data from many other people rather than find it all themselves. To write his laws of motion, Sir Isaac Newton built on the ideas and data of people who lived hundreds of years before him!

Today, scientists go through many years of school in order to study a certain kind of science for their job. Even with all their training, though, scientists can't be everywhere at once. They need help gathering data. That's where citizen scientists come in! They often play an important part in finding out more about the world around us.

Early citizen Scientists

Long ago, it was common for hunters to come together to shoot birds on Christmas Day. In 1900, a man named Frank M. Chapman suggested people count birds instead! The idea caught on! Today, Christmas bird counts are held across North America from mid-December to early January each year.

Chapman's idea to observe birds instead of shoot them turned an old holiday event into a new one. There's now over 100 years of data available on many North American bird populations.

Playing Games for Science

Foldit (fold.it/portal/) is an online game that lets ordinary people help scientists with their research! When playing Foldit, players are challenged to find the best ways to fold thousands of different **proteins**. Since there's a large number of ways to fold each protein, researchers invented the game to see what other people could come up with. The efforts of hundreds of thousands of players are helping to find cures for several health problems.

Mozak (www.mozak.science) is an online game in which players trace **neurons** to help scientists learn how our brains work. Stall Catchers (stallcatchers.com) lets players contribute to **Alzheimer's disease** research by finding blocked blood vessels.

Your Turn!

You can also contribute to brain research by playing one of the games at testmybrain.org. You'll have the chance to learn about yourself while playing memory games and taking speed-thinking tests! Your results will help scientists understand how the human mind works and how people think about the world around them.

Who knew playing computer games could help scientists?

9

Studying Insects

Researchers at the University of Minnesota are conducting a four-year study of the state's native bee population. The project is called the Minnesota Bee Atlas. Researchers have invited citizen scientists to help by sending in pictures and observations of their bee sightings.

Asian long-horned beetles are an invasive species responsible for killing thousands of trees in the United States. An invasive species is any nonnative animal or plant that is new to an area, spreads quickly, and is harmful. To help track and control these pests, citizens in New York are asked each summer to report when they find these beetles trapped in their swimming pools.

Asian long-horned beetle

Your Turn!

If you want to observe fast-moving insects, use a net to catch them. You can then place your catch in a glass jar with a lid. The jar let's you safely check out bugs while you do research to figure out what you've caught. Don't get stung or bitten!

Observations reported by citizen scientists can help researchers figure out where bee populations are growing and where they aren't.

Pollinators are animals that spread pollen, which helps plants make fruit and flowers. To study pollinator populations, people are being asked to join the Great Sunflower Project. So far, over 100,000 citizen scientists have taken part in the project by planting lemon queen sunflowers and reporting what pollinators visit their plants. The data collected helps researchers create maps that show where populations of pollinators, such as bees, are doing well and where they're weak.

The Monarch Larva Monitoring Project allows citizen scientists to help monarch butterflies. By observing monarch butterflies and reporting their findings, **volunteers** are helping scientists track monarch populations across North America.

Your Turn!

Do research to find out what insects migrate through your part of the country. Then collect data and pictures of those insects. Citizen science projects often have websites that explain how you can get involved, or take part, and what kind of data is needed. Visit monarchlab.org and www.greatsunflower.org for information about the projects on this page.

monarch butterfly

Scientists often call on their citizen scientists to take pictures. Pictures are needed to identify species, so they're very important!

13

The Solar Eclipse

A solar eclipse occurs when the moon passes between Earth and the sun, blocking the sun's light. On August 21, 2017, parts of North America experienced a total solar eclipse, which blocked all of the sun's light. Pictures of the eclipse taken by citizen scientists are helping researchers learn about the sun.

Citizen scientists also help researchers learn about how plants and animals are affected by eclipses. During a total eclipse in 1998, people reported fish that normally feed at night swimming out to look for food. In 1932, people in the northeastern United States reported flowers closing during a total eclipse.

Your Turn!

Will you be able to see the next solar eclipse where you live? Find a good viewing spot and make observations about plants and animals before, during, and after the eclipse. But remember to never look directly at the sun! Special glasses that protect your eyes when viewing an eclipse can be found online or at your local library or science museum.

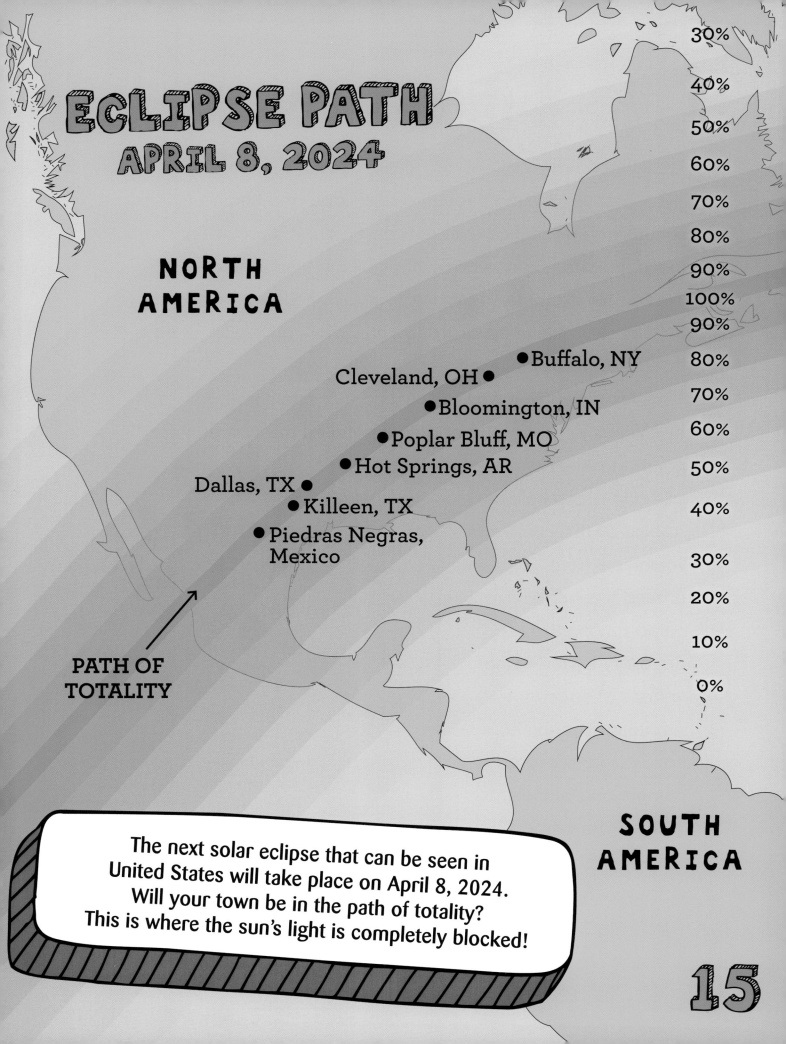

Making Space Discoveries

Imagine looking through a telescope and finding something no one has ever noticed before. Citizen scientists make important space discoveries all the time! Anthony Wesley, for example, is an **amateur** astronomer in Australia. In 2009, he discovered a strange new mark on Jupiter using a telescope he built himself.

Also in 2009, it was announced that scientists had discovered a new group of galaxies called the "Green Peas," named for their small size and green color. About 230,000 volunteers from around the world helped make this discovery by reviewing images of space. Amateur astronomers have also discovered **comets** and planets, such as Uranus!

Your Turn!

You can help NASA learn more about our universe! Visit science.nasa.gov/citizenscientists to learn about over 15 citizen scientist projects. You can report meteor sightings, sort through images from the Spitzer Space Telescope, or collect data about clouds in your area. Your efforts help NASA scientists measure, map, and better understand our galaxy.

Comet Hale-Bopp was discovered by Alan Hale, a **professional** astronomer, and Thomas Bopp, a construction worker with an interest in space!

Tracking Animal Populations

Keeping track of animal populations helps protect both the animals and their **environments**. If there are suddenly too many or too few of a certain kind of animal, it could be a sign that something's wrong. One way to track animal populations is to have groups of volunteers count animals in their area.

In Connecticut, citizen scientists help count large birds called osprey. People living near the Hudson River help scientists keep track of American eel populations. In 2014, volunteers counted 500 deer at Muddy Run Park in Holtwood, Pennsylvania. This was an increase from 2013, which showed the affect of a mild winter on the deer population.

Your Turn!

You and your friends can easily contribute to bird research. Scientists are trying to understand how people affect bird populations. The eBird Project collects citizen scientists' observations of different birds to study changes in population. Their website, ebird.org, explains all you need to know to record your sightings.

WHAT TO LOOK FOR WHEN OBSERVING ANIMALS IN NATURE

What are they doing?

Are they in a group or alone?

can you tell how old they are?

Do you notice them eating or trying to find food?

How quickly are they moving?

can you tell if they live nearby?

When you're observing wildlife, watch from a distance and be sure not to bother them!

Testing for Pollution

Modern steelmaking requires a fuel called coke. Coke is made from coal that's been heated to burn off **impurities**. The process of turning coal into coke creates pollution. People living near a coke plant in Tonawanda, New York, are worried that pollution from the plant may be making them sick.

In August 2017, volunteers in Tonawanda took small amounts of soil from around the community and sent them in for testing. Citizen scientists in the area had also been called on for soil samples 5 years earlier. When tested, the soil turned out to contain a number of dangerous chemicals.

air pollution in Paris, France

Smartphone Scientists

In 2015, citizen scientists all over Europe were invited to record air pollution levels using their smartphones. Using the iSpex app (ispex-eu.org/) and a small tool that connected to their phones, people recorded how pollution affected light in the air. The collected data helped scientists track air quality throughout Europe.

Using smartphone apps is an easy way to collect data and share it with scientists anywhere in the world!

Pet Projects

Some citizen science projects ask you to simply answer a few questions. One such project involves dogs. Each year thousands of people adopt dogs from animal shelters. The Dog Rehoming Project is working to improve the lives of shelter dogs through citizen science. You can help by answering questions on their website, www.thedogrehomingproject.org.

If cats are more your thing, Cat Tracker might be the project for you. You can take part by tracking your cat's movement using a **GPS** (Global Positioning System) device, answering questions about your pet's behavior, or sending in hair and food samples for a diet study. You can learn more at cattracker.org.

Your Turn!

There are some really interesting ways for you to take part in dog research! You can send in samples of your dog's spit to some projects. You can even mail in samples of your dog's poop! Other projects may ask you to send in a short video of you playing with your dog.

Playing with your dog can help scientists learn about man's best friend!

23

Weather Spotters

One of the easiest ways to be a citizen scientist is by observing the weather. Skywarn (www.skywarn.gov) is a group of about 290,000 citizen weather spotters. They share their observations with the National Weather Service (NWS). Information about severe storms, flooding, and hail from citizen scientists has saved lives!

The Cooperative Observer Program is an NWS program run by citizen scientists. Volunteers in many different environments collect and submit weather data including daily temperatures and rainfall and snowfall amounts. This data helps scientists measure changes in climate over long periods of time. You can find more information at www.nws.noaa.gov/om/coop/.

Your Turn!

You don't have to own expensive scientific instruments to collect weather data! With an adult's help, search online to find weather station projects you can build at home. Many projects are made from things found around the house. You can measure rain, snow and more. Don't forget to write down your observations!

What's the weather like where you are right now? You can report the weather with a smartphone using the mPing app (mping.nssl.noaa.gov/) and help the NWS improve their forecasts!

Climate Change

One of the biggest science subjects in the news today is **climate change**. Scientists have asked citizens for their help in many ways. In Fort Lauderdale, Florida, volunteers concerned with the effects of climate change on nesting sea turtles have been studying rising tides and increasing beach temperatures. In California, student volunteers are researching the effects of climate change on plants called ferns in redwood forests.

Citizen scientists are observing suckerfish that live in the Great Lakes. They're tracking migrations and also studying water quality. Changes in plant life, animal behavior, water quality, and tides give much-needed clues about changes in a region's climate.

Your Turn!

You can do your part to slow climate change! Most places have cleanup projects that need volunteers. If your school doesn't already take part in one, organize one yourself! Have a teacher help you gather interested students, parents, and teachers. Let your volunteers know where and when to meet, and get to work!

Pollution plays a part in climate change, so keeping your community free of grabage helps Earth!

Get Involved Today!

As a citizen scientist, you can be part of something big and important. The data you collect and share could help scientists better understand our planet. Everyone wants a cleaner world where we all live happily together. This is your chance to get involved! The data you collect could lead to important scientific discoveries.

Get your friends together for a citizen science project or take on one by yourself! There are many projects that only need quiet observation in nature, which means you can easily get started on your exciting adventure as a citizen scientist!

Your Turn!

You may be able to start a citizen science club at your school. Identify a teacher who you think would be the best to lead your club. Gather your friends who may also be interested and talk to your teacher about your ideas. Your teacher can help you get started.

What projects would you pick for your citizen science club? Citizen scientist activities are a fun way to spend time with your family and friends while making a difference!

GLOSSARY

Alzheimer's disease: a brain disease that causes memory loss, problems with thinking, and other harmful changes

amateur: someone who does something without pay

climate change: long-term change in Earth's climate caused partly by human activities such as burning oil and natural gas

comet: a space object made of ice and dust that has a long glowing tail when it passes close to the sun

environment: the conditions that surround a living thing and affect the way it lives

GPS: a system that uses satellite signals to locate places on Earth

impurity: something unwanted that is mixed in with a substance

neuron: a cell that carries messages between the brain and other body parts; the basic unit of the nervous system

professional: earning money from an activity that many people do for fun

protein: a necessary element found in all living things

species: a group of plants or animals that are all of the same kind

volunteer: a person who works without being paid

FOR MORE INFORMATION

BOOKS

Griffin Burns, Loree. *Citizen Scientists: Be a Part of Scientific Discovery from Your Own Backyard.* New York, NY: Henry Holt and Company, 2012.

Fontichiaro, Kristin. *Citizen Science.* Ann Arbor, MI: Cherry Lake Publishing, 2018.

Kovacs, Vic. *Get into Citizen Science.* New York, NY: Crabtree Publishing Company, 2017.

Landgraf, Greg. *Citizen Science Guide for Families: Taking Part in Real Science.* Chicago, IL: Huron Street Press, 2013.

WEBSITES

Citizen Science
www.eco-novice.com/2015/05/citizen-science-14-ways-your-family-can.html
Visit this website to find activities you and your family can do right in your own backyard!

Citizen Science Fun for All
pbskids.org/scigirls/citizen-science
This website is filled with citizen scientist projects for kids.

Test My Brain
testmybrain.org
Complete these fun online tests to help researchers learn more about how our brains work!